The Sign of the Beaver
Novel Literature Unit Study and Lapbook

Unit Study Created by Teresa Ives Lilly

www.hshighlights.com

This unit can be used in any grade level in which students are able to read the book. The activities are best used in grades 2 to 6. Almost everything in the unit can be used to create a file folder lap book. Each unit study covers one whole book and includes:

Comprehension Activities:
Fill in the Blanks, True and False, Multiple Choice, Who, What, Where, When, Why and How Questions.

Pre-Reading Skills Activities
Author Information Activity, Time line Activity, Theater Box Activity

Lesson Activities
Encyclopedia, Journal, Vocabulary, Sequence of Events, Handwriting Main Idea, Key Event, Prediction, Comparison,

Literature Skills Activity
Main Character, Main Setting, Main Problem, Possible Solutions, Character Traits, Character Interaction, Cause and Effect, Description, Pyramid of Importance, Villain vs. Hero

Poetry Skills Activity
Couplet, Triplet, Quinzain, Haiku, Cinquain, Tanka, Diamanté, Lantern and Shape Poem

Newspaper Writing Activity
Editorial, Travel, Advice Column, Comics, Society News, Sports, Obituary, Weddings, Book Review, Wanted Ads, Word Search

Creative Writing Activity
Letter, Fairy Tale, Mystery, Science Fiction, Fable, Dream or Nightmare, Tall Tale, Memoir, Newberry Award, A Different Ending.

Writing Skills Activity
Description, Expository, Dialogue, Process, Point of View, Persuasion, Compare and Contrast, Sequel, Climax and Plot Analysis.

Poster Board Activity
Collage, Theater Poster, Wanted Poster, Coat of Arms, Story Quilt, Chalk Art, Silhouette, Board Game Construction, Door Sign, Jeopardy.

Art Expression Activity
Main Character, Main Setting, Travel Brochure, Postal Stamp, Book Cover, Menu, Fashion Designer, Puzzle, Mini Book, Ten Commandments.

Creative Art Activity
Sculpture, Shadow Box, Mosaic, Mobile, Acrostic, Tapestry, Paper Dolls, Book Mark, Photography, Parade Float, Sketch

Other Activities:
Sign Language Vocabulary, Literature Web, Bingo.

How to do the Lapbook Activity: To use this unit study either print out all the pages or Student wills recreate most of them in a notebook or on white or colored paper.

All of the pages can be added to the lapbook project as shown in the photos, or only use those items you want to have students create a lapbook and have them use a spiral notebook for the other pages.

The following are photos of how the work can be presented in the lapbook format. To create the lapbook use 3-6 file folders (colored are best), construction paper or index cards, markers, glue and a stapler.

Front   Back

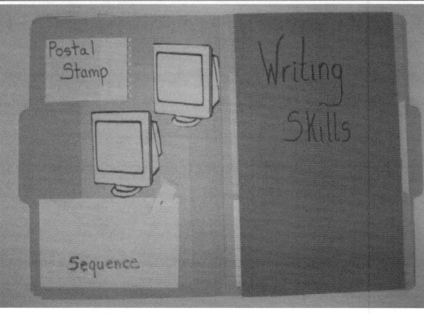

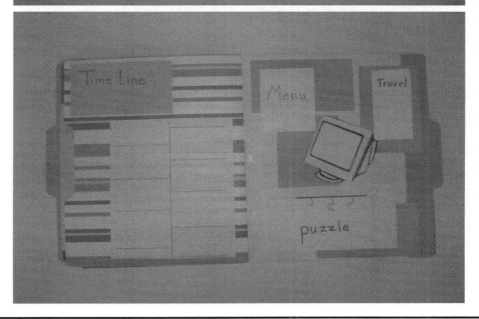

How to do the Newspaper Activity: As the student completes the news paper activities, have student lay the completed work out on a big board or on several poster boards. Don't have them glue the items on the board until the entire newspaper is completed and all sections are put where the student wants them to be. Have student create a name for their newspaper. Then have them type out the name, in big bold letters and place it on the top of the board. with tape or sticky clay. Then tape of stick all the completed articles onto board as well.

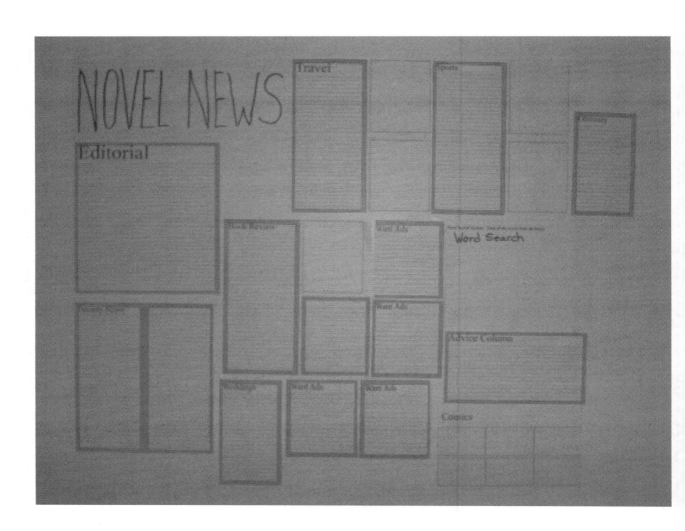

Pre-Reading
Activities

Pre-Reading Activity: Student will look at the book they will be studying for this unit. Then student will write the information required for this activity on the following book patterns or in their notebook. The patterns may be cut out and placed on the lapbook.

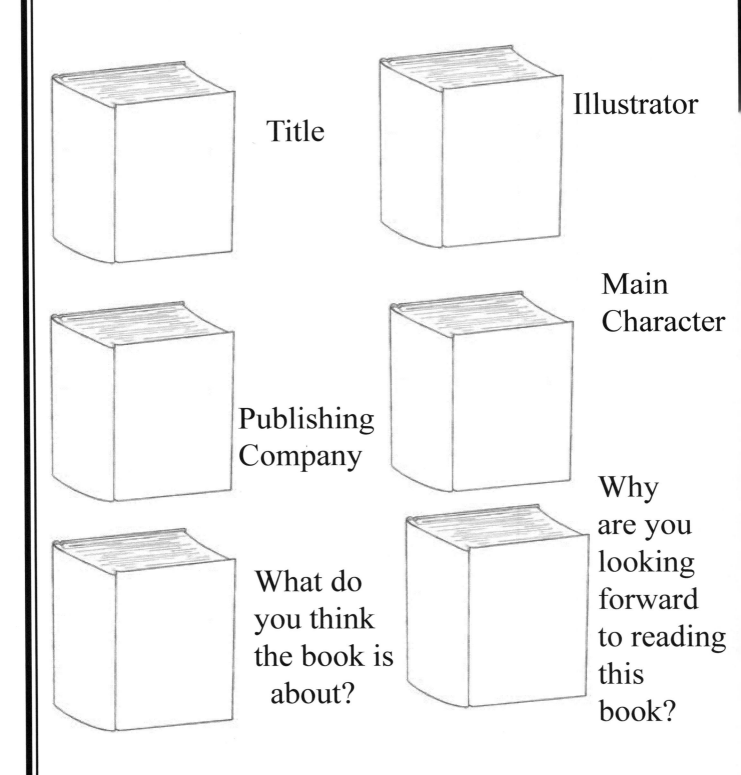

Title

Illustrator

Publishing Company

Main Character

What do you think the book is about?

Why are you looking forward to reading this book?

Author Activity: Student will use the book they are studying and information found on the internet to find out information about the author. Then student will write the information required for this activity on the patterns or in their notebook. The patterns may be cut out and placed on the lapbook.

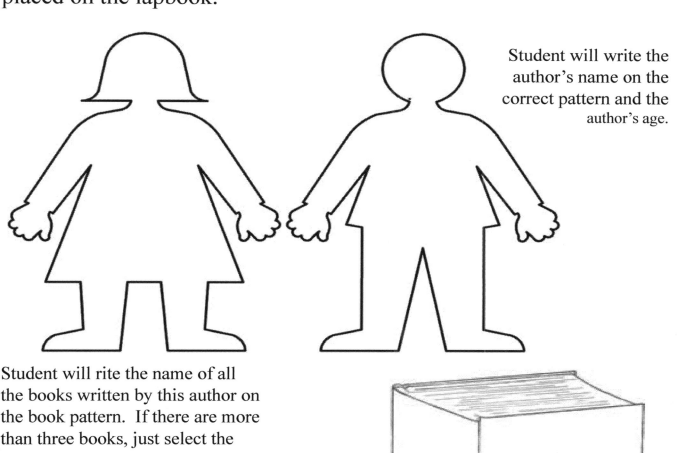

Student will write the author's name on the correct pattern and the author's age.

Student will rite the name of all the books written by this author on the book pattern. If there are more than three books, just select the three most famous.

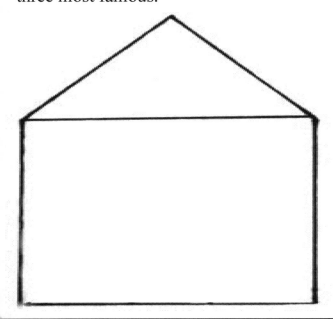

Student will write information about the author on the house pattern, such as where the author was born, lived and how they became an author.

Time Line Activity: Student will use the book they are studying to fill out the time line indicating when anything new, interesting or important happens in the book. This time line pattern can be copied into the student's notebook or this pattern can be printed smaller and placed on the lapbook.

All Vocabulary Lists, Comprehension Questions, True and False, Fill in the Blank for each lesson are at the end of this unit study.

Lesson 1
Activities

Lesson 1 Activities: Students will use the book they are studying and information found on the internet for the following activities. Then the student will write the information required for this activity on the patterns or in their notebook. The patterns may be cut out and placed on the lapbook.

Encyclopedia:
Student will choose one subject from this lesson that interested them and look it up on the internet or in encyclopedia. They will write the name of the subject across the top of the monitor pattern. On the monitor screen section, they will write three or more interesting facts about the subject.

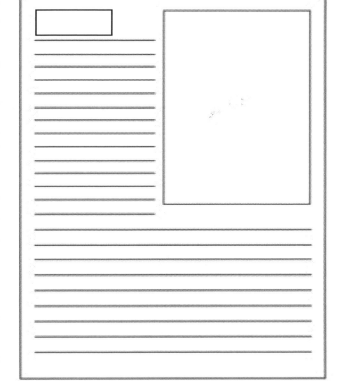

Journal:
Student will imagine that they are one of the characters from the story. After reading each lesson, they will write a short journal entry telling what happened from that character's point of view.
Student will also draw a picture to go along with the journal entry.
At the end of the book, student will staple all the journal entries together to form a complete booklet.
They can even create a special cover for it from construction paper.

Vocabulary word: _____
Definition of the word: _____
_____
_____

Antonym of the word: _____
How many syllables does the word have? _____

Vocabulary Word: _____
Sentence using the word: _____
_____
_____

Synonym of the word: _____

Vocabulary: Student will use the vocabulary words from the list for this lesson. On one of the patterns, or on one index card they will write one vocabulary word. They should also write the definition of the word, then the Antonym and how many Syllables the word has.

On the other card, the student will write the same word. They will write a full sentence using this word and then write the Synonym of the word.

They will repeat this for all the vocabulary words in this lesson.

Place the patterns or cards in an envelope which can be glued into the student's notebook or onto the lapbook..

Sequencing: At the end of the lesson the student will write two of the main events on these two strips. Save them in an envelope which can be glued onto the lapbook or in the notebook. At the end of the book, these strips can be taken out and the student can arrange them in the correct order as they occurred in the story.

Handwriting: Student will pick their favorite sentence that they read in this lesson. Have them write the sentence in their best handwriting on this page or in their notebook.

Student will write out the answers for the following:

Main Idea: In a sentence or two, write what the main idea was of this section.

_____

_____

_____

_____

_____

_____

Key Event: In a sentence or two write what the most important event was in this section.

_____

_____

_____

_____

_____

_____

_____

Prediction: In a sentence of two write what you Predict will happen in the next section.

_____

_____

_____

_____

_____

_____

Comparison: In a sentence of two compare two things in this section. Tell what makes them alike and what makes them different.

_____

_____

_____

_____

_____

_____

Fact or Opinion: In one sentence write a fact about this section and one sentence that is an opinion about the lesson.

_____

_____

_____

_____

_____

Literature Skills: **Main Character:** Student will write words in the circles to describe the main character.

Physical appearance

Concern or worry

Main character

Who they relate to

Your opinion of them

Poetry Form: Student will write a poem about the book or characters using this format.

Couplet: A Couplet is a two line poem with a fun and simple rhyming pattern. Each line has the same number of syllables and their endings must rhyme with one another. Humor is often used in couplets.

Example:
   If a seed could have its way
   it would grow in just one day.

Newspaper Activity: Student will use this form to write their newspaper piece on then paste it onto their newspaper lay out poster.

Editorial: An editorial is written by the editor of the newspaper. In an editorial the editor gives an opinion of something. Student will imagine that they are the editor of their newspaper. Student will write their opinion of something that happened in the book so far.

Editorial

Creative Writing Activity: Student will use this form or write in their notebook.
Letter Writing: Student will write a letter from one character in the book to another character in the book.

Dear   ,

Sincerely,

Writing Skills Activity: Student will use this form or write in their notebook.

Descriptive: Descriptive writing uses words such as color and texture to describe something. Student will describe a person, place or thing from the lesson.

_____

_____

_____

_____

_____

_____

_____

_____

_____

_____

_____

_____

_____

_____

_____

_____

_____

_____

_____

_____

_____

_____

_____

Lapbook Activity:

Main Character: Student will draw and color a picture of the main character on the solid section of the flap book. Student will cut out the entire flap book on the dotted lines and fold the four flap sections over the picture of the main character. On the outside of each flap student will write different words that describes the character; one word per flap.

Poster Board Activity:

Book Collage

Student will print out pictures from the internet that represent characters from the story. They can use magazine pictures as well. Then student will glue these pictures all over a 1/2 poster board in an over lapping fashion to create a book collage.

Creative Art Activity:

Sculpting

Student will create on of the characters from the story out of clay or play doe.

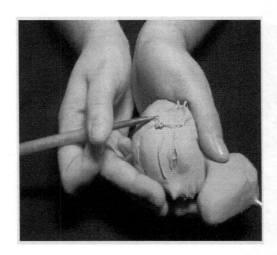

Lesson 2
Activities

Lesson 2 Activities: Students will use the book they are studying and information found on the internet for the following activities. Then the student will write the information required for this activity on the patterns or in their notebook. The patterns may be cut out and placed on the lapbook.

Encyclopedia:
Student will choose one subject from this lesson that interested them and look it up on the internet or in encyclopedia. They will write the name of the subject across the top of the monitor pattern. On the monitor screen section, they will write three or more interesting facts about the subject.

Journal:
Student will imagine that they are one of the characters from the story. After reading each lesson, they will write a short journal entry telling what happened from that character's point of view.
Student will also draw a picture to go along with the journal entry.
At the end of the book, student will staple all the journal entries together to form a complete booklet.
They can even create a special cover for it from construction paper.

Vocabulary word: _____

Definition of the word: _____

_____

_____

Antonym of the word: _____

How many syllables does the word have? _____

Vocabulary Word: _____

Sentence using the word: _____

_____

_____

Synonym of the word: _____

Vocabulary: Student will use the vocabulary words from the list for this lesson. On one of the patterns, or on one index card they will write one vocabulary word. They should also write the definition of the word, then the Antonym and how many Syllables the word has.

On the other card, the student will write the same word. They will write a full sentence using this word and then write the Synonym of the word.

They will repeat this for all the vocabulary words in this lesson.

Place the patterns or cards in an envelope which can be glued into the student's notebook or onto the lapbook..

Sequencing: At the end of the lesson the student will write two of the main events on these two strips. Save them in an envelope which can be glued onto the lapbook or in the notebook. At the end of the book, these strips can be taken out and the student can arrange them in the correct order as they occurred in the story.

Handwriting: Student will pick their favorite sentence that they read in this lesson. Have them write the sentence in their best handwriting on this page or in their notebook.

Student will write out the answers for the following:

Main Idea: In a sentence or two, write what the main idea was of this section.

_____
_____
_____
_____
_____
_____

Key Event: In a sentence or two write what the most important event was in this section.

_____
_____
_____
_____
_____
_____

Prediction: In a sentence of two write what you Predict will happen in the next section.

_____
_____
_____
_____
_____
_____

Comparison: In a sentence of two compare two things in this section. Tell what makes them alike and what makes them different.

_____
_____
_____
_____
_____

Fact or Opinion: In one sentence write a fact about this section and one sentence that is an opinion about the lesson.

_____
_____
_____
_____
_____
_____

Main Setting: Student will fill in the information to describe the main setting and to describe the minor settings in the story.

What is the main setting? _____

_____

Describe it _____

_____

_____

Describe a Minor Setting

_____

_____

_____

Describe a Minor Setting

_____

_____

_____

Poetry Form: Student will write a poem about the book or characters using this format.

Triplet:

Triplets are three-lined poems that rhyme.
Each line has the same number of
Syllables.

Example:
    The bunny hops and hops
    Til all at once she stops
    To munch some carrot tops.

_____

_____

_____

_____

_____

_____

_____

_____

Newspaper Activity: Student will use this form to write their newspaper piece on then paste it onto their newspaper lay out poster.

Travel Section: Student should imagine they write the travel column for a newspaper. Student should write a short article about traveling to the area where this book takes place. Student should find one or two photos on the internet that reminds them of this place and place it on the newspaper lay out poster as well.

Travel

Creative Writing Activity: Student will use this form or write in their notebook.

Fairy Tales : Fairy Tales are fanciful tales of legendary deeds and creatures, usually intended for children. Student will write a fairy tale involving one of the characters from the story and illustrate it.

Writing Skills Activity: Student will use this form or write in their notebook.

Persuasion: Persuasion is a way of writing, in which you convince someone of something. Student will write to try to persuade someone in the story to do something differently than they did in the story.

Lapbook Activity: **Main Setting** : Student will draw and color the main scene or main setting of this story for a play in this stage scene. Place in lapbook.

Poster Board Activity:
Theater Poster
Student will create a poster that may
be found outside of a theater which is putting
on a play of this book.

Creative Art Activity:
Shadow Box:
Student will use a shoe box
turned on its side to create a scene
from the book in using pictures from
the internet or other small items.

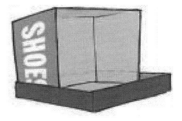

Lesson 3
Activities

Lesson 3 Activities: Students will use the book they are studying and information found on the internet for the following activities. Then the student will write the information required for this activity on the patterns or in their notebook. The patterns may be cut out and placed on the lapbook.

Encyclopedia:
Student will choose one subject from this lesson that interested them and look it up on the internet or in encyclopedia. They will write the name of the subject across the top of the monitor pattern. On the monitor screen section, they will write three or more interesting facts about the subject.

Journal:
Student will imagine that they are one of the characters from the story. After reading each lesson, they will write a short journal entry telling what happened from that character's point of view.
Student will also draw a picture to go along with the journal entry.
At the end of the book, student will staple all the journal entries together to form a complete booklet.
They can even create a special cover for it from construction paper.

Vocabulary word: _____
Definition of the word: _____
_____
_____

Antonym of the word: _____
How many syllables does the word have? _____

Vocabulary Word: _____
Sentence using the word: _____
_____
_____

Synonym of the word: _____

Vocabulary: Student will use the vocabulary words from the list for this lesson. On one of the patterns, or on one index card they will write one vocabulary word. They should also write the definition of the word, then the Antonym and how many Syllables the word has.

On the other card, the student will write the same word. They will write a full sentence using this word and then write the Synonym of the word.

They will repeat this for all the vocabulary words in this lesson.

Place the patterns or cards in an envelope which can be glued into the student's notebook or onto the lapbook..

Sequencing: At the end of the lesson the student will write two of the main events on these two strips. Save them in an envelope which can be glued onto the lapbook or in the notebook. At the end of the book, these strips can be taken out and the student can arrange them in the correct order as they occurred in the story.

Handwriting: Student will pick their favorite sentence that they read in this lesson. Have them write the sentence in their best handwriting on this page or in their notebook.

Student will write out the answers for the following:

Main Idea: In a sentence or two, write what the main idea was of this section.

_____
_____
_____
_____
_____
_____

Key Event: In a sentence or two write what the most important event was in this section.

_____
_____
_____
_____
_____
_____

Prediction: In a sentence of two write what you Predict will happen in the next section.

_____
_____
_____
_____
_____
_____

Comparison: In a sentence of two compare two things in this section. Tell what makes them alike and what makes them different.

_____
_____
_____
_____
_____

Fact or Opinion: In one sentence write a fact about this section and one sentence that is an opinion about the lesson.

_____
_____
_____
_____
_____

Main Problem: Most stories seem to have one main problem. There may be other small problems, but there is an overall large problem. Student will write what the main problem is in the larger rectangle, and some of the smaller problems in the smaller ones.

Poetry Form: Student will write a poem about the book or characters using this format.

Quinzain: Quinzains are unrhymed three line poems that contain 15 syllables. The pattern is: The first line is 7, the second is 5 and the third is 3. The first line makes a statement and the next two lines ask a question about the subject.

Example:
    I like to write poetry
    would you like to write
    a poem too?

Newspaper Activity: Student will use this form to write their newspaper piece on then paste it onto their newspaper lay out poster.

Wanted Ads Section: Student will create several wanted ads that characters in the story might post in a newspaper or ads the characters might answer.

Wanted Ad

Wanted Ad

Wanted Ad

Wanted Ad

Creative Writing Activity: Student will use this form or write in their notebook.

Mystery: Student will write a mystery that may occur in this story or to the characters in this story and then illustrate it.

Writing Skills Activity: Student will use this form or write in their notebook.

Expository: Expository writing is writing strictly to inform. Student will write an expository piece that informs someone about an event that happened in the story.

_____

- -

_____

_____

- -

_____

_____

- -

_____

_____

- -

_____

_____

- -

_____

_____

- -

_____

_____

- -

_____

_____

- -

_____

Lapbook Activity: **Travel Brochure**: Student will use this form to create a travel brochure on. It should describe a place in the story that people should come to visit. Student may use pictures from the internet if necessary.

Poster Board Activity:
Wanted Poster
Student will create a "Wanted by the Law," poster for one of the villains in the story.

Creative Art Activity:
Mosaic Plate
Student will create a mosaic scene from the story on a paper plate using small pieces of construction paper glued in a mosaic fashion.

Lesson 4
Activities

Lesson 4 Activities: Students will use the book they are studying and information found on the internet for the following activities. Then the student will write the information required for this activity on the patterns or in their notebook. The patterns may be cut out and placed on the lapbook.

Encyclopedia:
Student will choose one subject from this lesson that interested them and look it up on the internet or in encyclopedia. They will write the name of the subject across the top of the monitor pattern. On the monitor screen section, they will write three or more interesting facts about the subject.

Journal:
Student will imagine that they are one of the characters from the story. After reading each lesson, they will write a short journal entry telling what happened from that character's point of view.
Student will also draw a picture to go along with the journal entry.
At the end of the book, student will staple all the journal entries together to form a complete booklet.
They can even create a special cover for it from construction paper.

Vocabulary word: _____
Definition of the word: _____
_____
_____

Antonym of the word: _____
How many syllables does the word have? _____

Vocabulary Word: _____
Sentence using the word: _____
_____
_____

Synonym of the word: _____

Vocabulary: Student will use the vocabulary words from the list for this lesson. On one of the patterns, or on one index card they will write one vocabulary word. They should also write the definition of the word, then the Antonym and how many Syllables the word has.

On the other card, the student will write the same word. They will write a full sentence using this word and then write the Synonym of the word.

They will repeat this for all the vocabulary words in this lesson.

Place the patterns or cards in an envelope which can be glued into the student's notebook or onto the lapbook..

Sequencing: At the end of the lesson the student will write two of the main events on these two strips. Save them in an envelope which can be glued onto the lapbook or in the notebook. At the end of the book, these strips can be taken out and the student can arrange them in the correct order as they occurred in the story.

Handwriting: Student will pick their favorite sentence that they read in this lesson. Have them write the sentence in their best handwriting on this page or in their notebook.

Student will write out the answers for the following:

Main Idea: In a sentence or two, write what the main idea was of this section.

_____
_____
_____
_____
_____
_____

Key Event: In a sentence or two write what the most important event was in this section.

_____
_____
_____
_____
_____
_____

Prediction: In a sentence of two write what you Predict will happen in the next section.

_____
_____
_____
_____
_____
_____

Comparison: In a sentence of two compare two things in this section. Tell what makes them alike and what makes them different.

_____
_____
_____
_____
_____

Fact or Opinion: In one sentence write a fact about this section and one sentence that is an opinion about the lesson.

_____
_____
_____
_____
_____

Possible Solutions: Problems in a story can have several solutions. Student will write what some of the problems are in the story and possible solution in the shapes.

Problem:

Solution:

Problem:

Solution:

Problem:

Solution:

Poetry Form: Student will write a poem about the book or characters using this format.

Haiku: A haiku is a Japanese poem with no rhyme. Haiku poems have only three lines, each with a certain number of syllables.

Here is the pattern:
Line 1 = 5 syllables
Line 2 = 7 syllables
Line 3 = 5 syllables

Example:
Lion cubs doze in
shade, under shrubs, hidden from
hungry hyenas

Newspaper Activity: Student will use this form to write their newspaper piece on then paste it onto their newspaper lay out poster.

Advice Column Section: Student will come up with a question or concern that one of the characters in the story may have. The student will write a letter to the advice column and the advice column writer will answer.

Advice Column

Creative Writing Activity: Student will use this form or write in their notebook.

Science Fiction: Science Fiction stories take place in the far future usually in space or on earth in an advanced society. Student will write a science fiction story about the future of one of the characters and illustrate it.

Writing Skills Activity: Student will use this form or write in their notebook.

Dialogue: A dialogue is a conversation between two characters. Student will write a dialogue that could occur between two characters in the story. Student should use correct quotation marks.

_____

_____

_____

_____

_____

_____

_____

_____

_____

_____

_____

_____

_____

_____

_____

_____

_____

_____

_____

_____

_____

_____

_____

_____

_____

Lapbook Activity: Postal Stamp: Student will create a new postal stamp for next year which would represent the book or characters of the book.

Poster Board Activity:
Coat of Arms
Using a poster board, student will create a coat of arms with a design to represent this story or a character in the story.

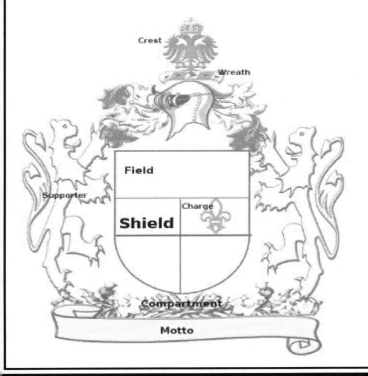

Creative Art Activity:
Mobile
Student will cut out pictures from the internet of characters of items that represent those in the book and then glue them onto long strips of card board. These can be hung with string to make a mobile.

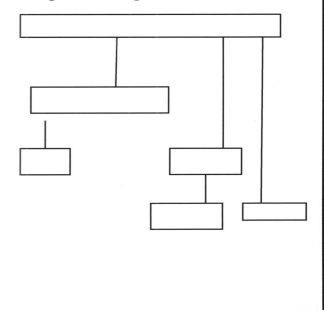

Lesson 5
Activities

Lesson 5 Activities: Students will use the book they are studying and information found on the internet for the following activities. Then the student will write the information required for this activity on the patterns or in their notebook. The patterns may be cut out and placed on the lapbook.

Encyclopedia:
Student will choose one subject from this lesson that interested them and look it up on the internet or in encyclopedia. They will write the name of the subject across the top of the monitor pattern. On the monitor screen section, they will write three or more interesting facts about the subject.

Journal:
Student will imagine that they are one of the characters from the story. After reading each lesson, they will write a short journal entry telling what happened from that character's point of view.
Student will also draw a picture to go along with the journal entry.
At the end of the book, student will staple all the journal entries together to form a complete booklet.
They can even create a special cover for it from construction paper.

Vocabulary word: _____
Definition of the word: _____
_____
_____

Antonym of the word: _____
How many syllables does the word have? _____

Vocabulary Word: _____
Sentence using the word: _____
_____
_____

Synonym of the word: _____

Vocabulary: Student will use the vocabulary words from the list for this lesson. On one of the patterns, or on one index card they will write one vocabulary word. They should also write the definition of the word, then the Antonym and how many Syllables the word has.

On the other card, the student will write the same word. They will write a full sentence using this word and then write the Synonym of the word.

They will repeat this for all the vocabulary words in this lesson.

Place the patterns or cards in an envelope which can be glued into the student's notebook or onto the lapbook..

Sequencing: At the end of the lesson the student will write two of the main events on these two strips. Save them in an envelope which can be glued onto the lapbook or in the notebook. At the end of the book, these strips can be taken out and the student can arrange them in the correct order as they occurred in the story.

Handwriting: Student will pick their favorite sentence that they read in this lesson. Have them write the sentence in their best handwriting on this page or in their notebook.

Student will write out the answers for the following:

Main Idea: In a sentence or two, write what the main idea was of this section.

_____
_____
_____
_____
_____
_____

Key Event: In a sentence or two write what the most important event was in this section.

_____
_____
_____
_____
_____
_____

Prediction: In a sentence of two write what you Predict will happen in the next section.

_____
_____
_____
_____
_____
_____

Comparison: In a sentence of two compare two things in this section. Tell what makes them alike and what makes them different.

_____
_____
_____
_____
_____

Fact or Opinion: In one sentence write a fact about this section and one sentence that is an opinion about the lesson.

_____
_____
_____
_____
_____

Character Traits: In the circle for the Main Character Traits, student will write several of the main character's traits. In the circle for Student Traits, student will write several of the student's traits. Any traits that the main character and the student have in common should be in the area where the circles overlap called Common Traits.

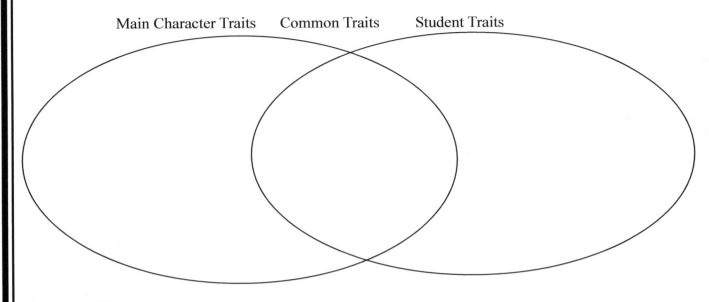

Main Character Traits   Common Traits   Student Traits

Poetry Form: Student will write a poem about the book or characters using this format.

Acrostic: In an acrostic poem the name of the person, object, or place is written vertically down the left hand side of the page. Each letter is capitalized and becomes the first letter of the word beginning each line. The words used should describe the person, object or place in a positive way. Each line may comprise a word, a phrase or a thought that is continued on to the next line.

> Example:
>
> CAT
> Can you see their eyes
> At night in the dark
> They glow........

_____
_____
_____
_____
_____
_____
_____
_____
_____
_____
_____
_____
_____

Newspaper Activity: Student will use this form to write their newspaper piece on then paste it onto their newspaper lay out poster.

Comic Section: Student will create a funny cartoon about one of the events of characters in the story. Illustrate and color it.

Comics

Creative Writing Activity: Student will use this form or write in their notebook.
Fable: A fable is a short, allegorical narrative, making a moral point, traditionally by means of animal characters that speak and act like humans. Student will write a fable that comes to mind while reading this story in which one of the characters from the book learns a moral from an animal. Then student will illustrate it.

Writing Skills Activity: Student will use this form or write in their notebook.

Process: Process writing is telling the actual steps it takes to do something. Student will write a step by step process that one of the characters in the book had to do to or should have done.

_____

- -

_____

_____

- -

_____

_____

- -

_____

_____

- -

_____

_____

- -

_____

_____

- -

_____

_____

- -

_____

_____

- -

_____

Lapbook Activity: Book Cover Illustrator: Student will create their own book cover for this story on the form. Make sure to include the title, illustrator and publisher's name.

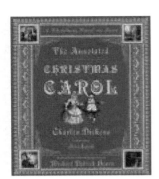

Poster Board Activity:
Story Quilt
Divide a poster board into eight to sixteen equal squares. In each square the student will draw different pictures to tell what has happened in the story so far.

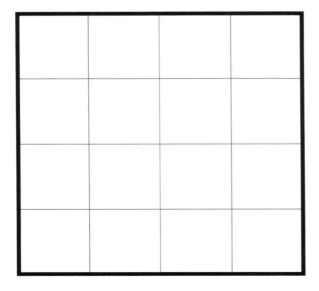

Creative Art Activity:
Tapestry
Using an 8 inch by 12 inch piece of felt as the background, student will cut out characters and items from the story from colored felt and glue onto the background to create a story tapestry.

Lesson 6
Activities

Lesson 6 Activities: Students will use the book they are studying and information found on the internet for the following activities. Then the student will write the information required for this activity on the patterns or in their notebook. The patterns may be cut out and placed on the lapbook.

Encyclopedia:
Student will choose one subject from this lesson that interested them and look it up on the internet or in encyclopedia. They will write the name of the subject across the top of the monitor pattern. On the monitor screen section, they will write three or more interesting facts about the subject.

Journal:
Student will imagine that they are one of the characters from the story. After reading each lesson, they will write a short journal entry telling what happened from that character's point of view.
Student will also draw a picture to go along with the journal entry.
At the end of the book, student will staple all the journal entries together to form a complete booklet.
They can even create a special cover for it from construction paper.

Vocabulary word: _____
Definition of the word: _____
_____
_____

Antonym of the word: _____
How many syllables does the word have? _____

Vocabulary Word: _____
Sentence using the word: _____
_____
_____

Synonym of the word: _____

Vocabulary: Student will use the vocabulary words from the list for this lesson. On one of the patterns, or on one index card they will write one vocabulary word. They should also write the definition of the word, then the Antonym and how many Syllables the word has.

On the other card, the student will write the same word. They will write a full sentence using this word and then write the Synonym of the word.

They will repeat this for all the vocabulary words in this lesson.

Place the patterns or cards in an envelope which can be glued into the student's notebook or onto the lapbook..

Sequencing: At the end of the lesson the student will write two of the main events on these two strips. Save them in an envelope which can be glued onto the lapbook or in the notebook. At the end of the book, these strips can be taken out and the student can arrange them in the correct order as they occurred in the story.

Handwriting: Student will pick their favorite sentence they read in this lesson. Have them write the sentence in their best handwriting on this page or in their notebook.

Student will write out the answers for the following:

Main Idea: In a sentence or two, write what the main idea was of this section.

_____
_____
_____
_____
_____
_____

Key Event: In a sentence or two write what the most important event was in this section.

_____
_____
_____
_____
_____
_____

Prediction: In a sentence of two write what you Predict will happen in the next section.

_____
_____
_____
_____
_____
_____

Comparison: In a sentence of two compare two things in this section. Tell what makes them alike and what makes them different.

_____
_____
_____
_____
_____

Fact or Opinion: In one sentence write a fact about this section and one sentence that is an opinion about the lesson.

_____
_____
_____
_____
_____

Character Interaction:
In the circles, student will write the names of the characters in the story and then draw arrows from each circle to other circles to represent which character interact with one another. Start with the Main Character in the center.

Poetry Form:
Student will write a poem about the book or characters using this format.

Cinquain: A cinquain is a short, five-line, non rhyming poem which follows the following pattern:

First line - The title (one word)
2nd line - Describes the title (two words)
3rd line - Express action (three words)
4th line - A feeling or thought (four words)
5th line - A Synonym or close word for the title

Example:
Insect
six legs
usually have wings
a mostly helpful annoyance
Bee

Newspaper Activity: Student will use this form to write their newspaper piece on then paste it onto their newspaper lay out poster.

Obituary Section: Student will imagine that one or more of the characters in the book died and will write an obituary telling how they died.

Wedding Announcement Section: Student will imagine that one of the characters in the story will get married soon and will write the wedding announcement, telling who they will marry, where and when the wedding will take place.

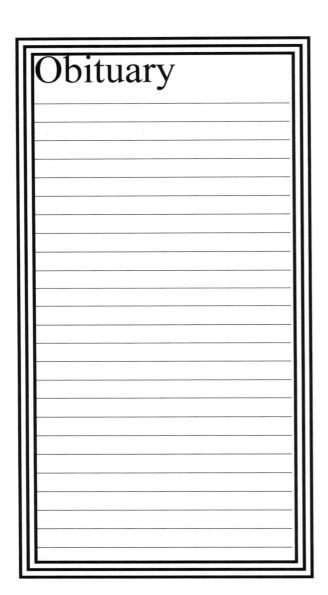

Obituary

Weddings

Creative Writing Activity: Dream or Nightmare: Student will write a dream or nightmare one of the characters in the story may have, and illustrate it.

Writing Skills Activity: Student will use this form or write in their notebook.

Point of View: Point of View is telling a story from one person's view. Student will write about an event in this story from a different character's point of view.

_____

- -

_____

- -

_____

- -

_____

- -

_____

- -

_____

- -

_____

- -

_____

- -

_____

- -

_____

- -

_____

- -

_____

- -

_____

- -

_____

- -

_____

Lapbook Activity: Menu: Student will create a menu for a restaurant that the characters in the book may have owned or eaten at. Student will decorate the front of the menu in an interesting and inviting fashion.

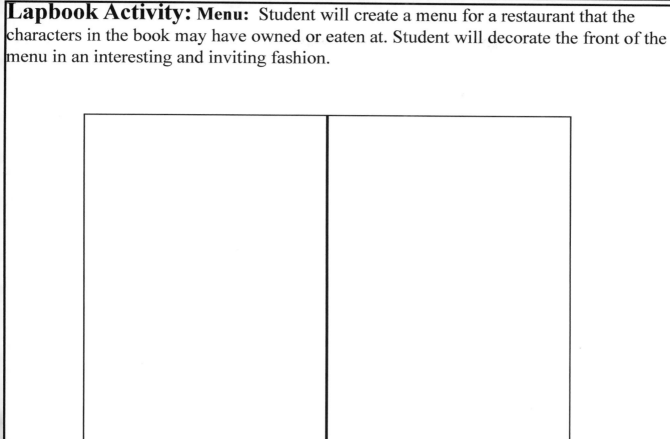

Poster Board Activity:
Chalk Art
On a black poster board student will use colored chalk to illustrate a scene or event in the story.

Creative Art Activity:
Paper Doll
Student will cut out pictures from the internet of people to represent the characters in this story and then laminate them and glue them onto sticks. Students can use them to act out parts of the story or the dialogue the student wrote in an earlier lesson.

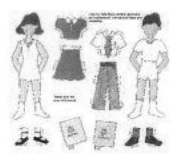

Lesson 7
Activities

Lesson 7 Activities: Students will use the book they are studying and information found on the internet for the following activities. Then the student will write the information required for this activity on the patterns or in their notebook. The patterns may be cut out and placed on the lapbook.

Encyclopedia:
Student will choose one subject from this lesson that interested them and look it up on the internet or in encyclopedia. They will write the name of the subject across the top of the monitor pattern. On the monitor screen section, they will write three or more interesting facts about the subject.

Journal:
Student will imagine that they are one of the characters from the story. After reading each lesson, they will write a short journal entry telling what happened from that character's point of view.
Student will also draw a picture to go along with the journal entry.
At the end of the book, student will staple all the journal entries together to form a complete booklet.
They can even create a special cover for it from construction paper.

Vocabulary word: _____
Definition of the word: _____
_____
_____

Antonym of the word: _____
How many syllables does the word have? _____

Vocabulary Word: _____
Sentence using the word: _____
_____
_____

Synonym of the word: _____

Vocabulary: Student will use the vocabulary words from the list for this lesson. On one of the patterns, or on one index card they will write one vocabulary word. They should also write the definition of the word, then the Antonym and how many Syllables the word has.

On the other card, the student will write the same word. They will write a full sentence using this word and then write the Synonym of the word.

They will repeat this for all the vocabulary words in this lesson.

Place the patterns or cards in an envelope which can be glued into the student's notebook or onto the lapbook..

Sequencing: At the end of the lesson the student will write two of the main events on these two strips. Save them in an envelope which can be glued onto the lapbook or in the notebook. At the end of the book, these strips can be taken out and the student can arrange them in the correct order as they occurred in the story.

Handwriting: Student will pick their favorite sentence that they read in this lesson. Have them write the sentence in their best handwriting on this page or in their notebook.

Student will write out the answers for the following:

Main Idea: In a sentence or two, write what the main idea was of this section.

_____
_____
_____
_____
_____

Key Event: In a sentence or two write what the most important event was in this section.

_____
_____
_____
_____
_____

Prediction: In a sentence of two write what you Predict will happen in the next section.

_____
_____
_____
_____
_____

Comparison: In a sentence of two compare two things in this section. Tell what makes them alike and what makes them different.

_____
_____
_____
_____
_____

Fact or Opinion: In one sentence write a fact about this section and one sentence that is an opinion about the lesson.

_____
_____
_____
_____
_____

Cause and Effect: When one thing happens in a story, many other things happen because of this one event. This is called cause and effect. In the center circle, student will write one thing that happened in the story (the cause). In the smaller circles, student will write the variety of things that happened because of that main cause (the effects).

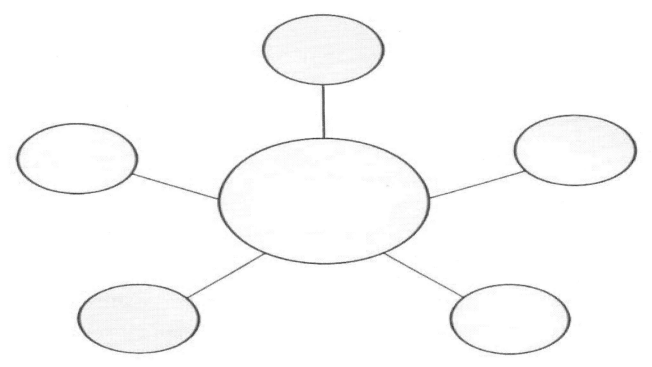

Poetry Form: Student will write a poem about the book or characters using this format.

Tanka: A Tanka is a form of Japanese poetry that depends on the number of lines and syllables instead of rhyme. The pattern is:
Line 1 = 5 syllables, Line 2 = 7 syllables
Line 3 = 5 syllables, Line 4 = 7 syllables
Line 5 = 7 syllables

Example:
  Blue-eyed baby cubs
  wobble out of winter's den
  warm sun on cold fur
  forest smells of fresh, cold pine
  wild, new world to grow into.

Newspaper Activity: Student will use this form to write their newspaper piece on then paste it onto their newspaper lay out poster.

Society News Section: Student will write about someone in the story who would be considered a fairly famous person or character. Write a society column about an event or party that they may have attended.

Society News

Creative Writing Activity: Tall Tales: Tall tales are humorous, exaggerated stories common on the American frontier. Student will write a tall tale about one of the characters in the story and then illustrate it.

Writing Skills Activity: Student will use this form or write in their notebook.

Compare and Contrast: Compare and Contrast tell about two or more things and how they are alike or different. Student will write to Compare and Contrast two characters in the story.

_____

- -

_____

_____

- -

_____

_____

- -

_____

_____

- -

_____

_____

- -

_____

_____

- -

_____

_____

- -

_____

_____

- -

_____

Lapbook Activity: Fashion Designer: Student will design clothing that one or more of the characters in the story would have worn. Student will color them or cut them out of scraps of material and put them on the doll form that represents the character and then attach to lapbook.

Poster Board Activity:
Silhouette
Using black construction paper, student will cut out a silhouette of the main character or an item from the story and glue it onto the center of a white or colored 1/2 poster board. Then student will create a frame around the outside with a black poster board.

Creative Art Activity:
Book Mark
Using thick tag board, student will cut into a rectangle 3 inches by 6 inches, and create a book mark that resembles something about the book. Then student will punch a hole in the end and tie ribbon or string through it. Laminate it if possible.

Lesson 8
Activities

Lesson 8 Activities: Students will use the book they are studying and information found on the internet for the following activities. Then the student will write the information required for this activity on the patterns or in their notebook. The patterns may be cut out and placed on the lapbook.

Encyclopedia:
Student will choose one subject from this lesson that interested them and look it up on the internet or in encyclopedia. They will write the name of the subject across the top of the monitor pattern. On the monitor screen section, they will write three or more interesting facts about the subject.

Journal:
Student will imagine that they are one of the characters from the story. After reading each lesson, they will write a short journal entry telling what happened from that character's point of view.
Student will also draw a picture to go along with the journal entry.
At the end of the book, student will staple all the journal entries together to form a complete booklet.
They can even create a special cover for it from construction paper.

Vocabulary word: _____
Definition of the word: _____
_____
_____

Antonym of the word: _____
How many syllables does the word have? _____

Vocabulary Word: _____
Sentence using the word: _____
_____
_____

Synonym of the word: _____

Vocabulary: Student will use the vocabulary words from the list for this lesson. On one of the patterns, or on one index card they will write one vocabulary word. They should also write the definition of the word, then the Antonym and how many Syllables the word has.

On the other card, the student will write the same word. They will write a full sentence using this word and then write the Synonym of the word.

They will repeat this for all the vocabulary words in this lesson.

Place the patterns or cards in an envelope which can be glued into the student's notebook or onto the lapbook..

Sequencing: At the end of the lesson the student will write two of the main events on these two strips. Save them in an envelope which can be glued onto the lapbook or in the notebook. At the end of the book, these strips can be taken out and the student can arrange them in the correct order as they occurred in the story.

_____
_____
_____
_____
_____
_____

Handwriting: Student will pick their favorite sentence that they read in this lesson. Have them write the sentence in their best handwriting on this page or in their notebook.

Student will write out the answers for the following:

Main Idea: In a sentence or two, write what the main idea was of this section.

_____
_____
_____
_____
_____
_____

Key Event: In a sentence or two write what the most important event was in this section.

_____
_____
_____
_____
_____
_____

Prediction: In a sentence of two write what you Predict will happen in the next section.

_____
_____
_____
_____
_____
_____

Comparison: In a sentence of two compare two things in this section. Tell what makes them alike and what makes them different.

_____
_____
_____
_____
_____
_____

Fact or Opinion: In one sentence write a fact about this section and one sentence that is an opinion about the lesson.

_____
_____
_____
_____
_____
_____

Descriptions: Authors use descriptive words so that the reader can imagine the place or thing that is being described. Student will find one place in the book that the author really described well and write the name of the place inside the polygon. On the lines coming out of the polygon, student will write the words the author used to describe the place such as pretty, dark, blue....

Poetry Form: Student will write a poem about the book or characters using this format.

Diamanté: A diamanté is a seven-line, diamond-shaped poem which contrasts two opposites. The pattern is: First Line and seventh line - Name the opposites. Second and sixth lines - Two adjectives describing the opposite nearest it. Third and fifth lines - Three participles (ing words) describing the nearest opposite. Fourth line - two nouns for each of the opposites.

Example:	Fish
	silvered, baited
	teeming, swimming, darting
	scaled amphibian, graceful hind
	running, leaping, grazing
	hunted, mammal
	Deer

Newspaper Activity: Student will use this form to write their newspaper piece on then paste it onto their newspaper lay out poster.

Sports Section: Student will imagine that one of the characters in your book is in a sports competition and write a newspaper article about it and then illustrate it as well.

Sports

Creative Writing Activity: Memoir: When writing a memoir, a person chooses one time or one event and expounds upon it by stretching the truth. Student will write a memoir as if they were a character in the story. They should choose one event to write about, and stretch the truth in the retelling.

My Memoir

_____

_____

_____

_____

_____

_____

_____

_____

_____

_____

_____

_____

_____

_____

_____

_____

_____

_____

_____

_____

_____

_____

_____

_____

_____

_____

_____

_____

_____

_____

_____

_____

Writing Skills Activity: Student will use this form or write in their notebook.

Sequel: A sequel is a movie or book that follows another. The sequel contains the same characters and follows the same story line. The characters and story line may change during the sequel but they have to start out the same to show the connection with the previous story. Students will write the first few paragraphs of a sequel for this story.

_____

- -

_____

_____

- -

_____

_____

- -

_____

_____

- -

_____

_____

- -

_____

_____

- -

_____

_____

- -

_____

_____

- -

_____

Lapbook Activity: Book Cover Puzzle:

Student will glue a picture they print from the internet of the book cover, onto this puzzle pattern so that the pattern shows on the back. Then student will cut the book cover into puzzle pieces. This can go in an envelope on the lapbook to be put together later.

Poster Board Activity:
Board Game
Student will create a board game on the poster board to use with this story.

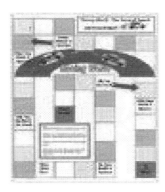

Creative Art Activity:
Photography
Photography is a great form of art. Student will find things that reminds them of this book and take some photos of it. Get these printed in black and white and some in color. Student can turn these into cards, frame them or take photos of one item in different angles and create a unique photo like this one.

Lesson 9
Activity

Lesson 9 Activities: Students will use the book they are studying and information found on the internet for the following activities. Then the student will write the information required for this activity on the patterns or in their notebook. The patterns may be cut out and placed on the lapbook.

Encyclopedia:
Student will choose one subject from this lesson that interested them and look it up on the internet or in encyclopedia. They will write the name of the subject across the top of the monitor pattern. On the monitor screen section, they will write three or more interesting facts about the subject.

Journal:
Student will imagine that they are one of the characters from the story. After reading each lesson, they will write a short journal entry telling what happened from that character's point of view.
Student will also draw a picture to go along with the journal entry.
At the end of the book, student will staple all the journal entries together to form a complete booklet.
They can even create a special cover for it from construction paper.

Vocabulary word: _____

Definition of the word: _____

_____

_____

Antonym of the word: _____

How many syllables does the word have? _____

Vocabulary Word: _____

Sentence using the word: _____

_____

_____

Synonym of the word: _____

_____
_____
_____

_____
_____
_____

Vocabulary: Student will use the vocabulary words from the list for this lesson. On one of the patterns, or on one index card they will write one vocabulary word. They should also write the definition of the word, then the Antonym and how many Syllables the word has.

On the other card, the student will write the same word. They will write a full sentence using this word and then write the Synonym of the word.

They will repeat this for all the vocabulary words in this lesson.

Place the patterns or cards in an envelope which can be glued into the student's notebook or onto the lapbook..

Sequencing: At the end of the lesson the student will write two of the main events on these two strips. Save them in an envelope which can be glued onto the lapbook or in the notebook. At the end of the book, these strips can be taken out and the student can arrange them in the correct order as they occurred in the story.

Handwriting: Student will pick their favorite sentence that they read in this lesson. Have them write the sentence in their best handwriting on this page or in their notebook.

Student will write out the answers for the following:

Main Idea: In a sentence or two, write what the main idea was of this section.

_____
_____
_____
_____
_____

Key Event: In a sentence or two write what the most important event was in this section.

_____
_____
_____
_____
_____

Prediction: In a sentence of two write what you Predict will happen in the next section.

_____
_____
_____
_____
_____

Comparison: In a sentence of two compare two things in this section. Tell what makes them alike and what makes them different.

_____
_____
_____
_____

Fact or Opinion: In one sentence write a fact about this section and one sentence that is an opinion about the lesson.

_____
_____
_____
_____

Pyramid of Importance: Each character in the story holds a position of importance. Some are of main importance, some are of less importance. Student will fill in the pyramid with the names of the characters. The top should have the most important character, the next line the next most important characters and continue down until you have listed all the characters in order of importance.

Poetry Form: Student will write a poem about the book or characters using this format.

Lantern: A lantern is a five line poem in the shape of a Japanese lantern. The Pattern is:

Line 1: noun (one syllable)
Line 2: describe the noun (two syllables)
Line 3: describe the noun (three syllables
Line 4: describe the noun (four syllables)
Line 5: Synonym for noun in line one (one syllable)

Example:	Mane
	long, thick
	blonde to black
	royal mantle
	Fur

Newspaper Activity: Student will use this form to write their newspaper piece on then paste it onto their newspaper lay out poster.

Entertainment Section: Book Review Student will write an over all review of the book and tell what they liked and did not like, which characters seemed real and which scenes were described the best. Student should also ad a picture of the book cover.

Book Review

Creative Writing Activity: Newberry Award: Each year one book is chosen to receive the John Newberry Award for great writing. Student will write a short report on why this book did or should have won the award.

Writing Skills Activity: Student will use this form or write in their notebook.

Climax: The climax of a story is the point where the reader knows who wins the conflict or how the problem will be solved. Student will write what the main problem was and at what point they knew how it would be solved.

_____

_____

_____

_____

_____

_____

_____

_____

_____

_____

_____

_____

_____

_____

_____

_____

_____

_____

_____

_____

_____

_____

_____

Lapbook Activity: Mini Book: Student will make a mini book about this story or about a subject in the story. See the pattern on one of the following pages.

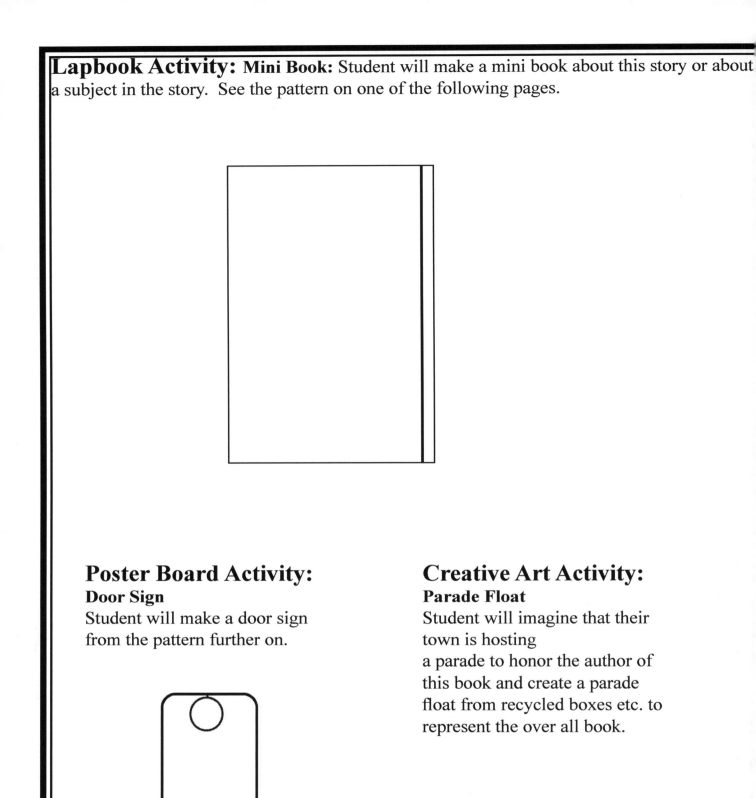

Poster Board Activity:
Door Sign
Student will make a door sign from the pattern further on.

Creative Art Activity:
Parade Float
Student will imagine that their town is hosting a parade to honor the author of this book and create a parade float from recycled boxes etc. to represent the over all book.

Door Sign: On a piece of poster board student will create a sign for their bedroom door that represents something from the book.

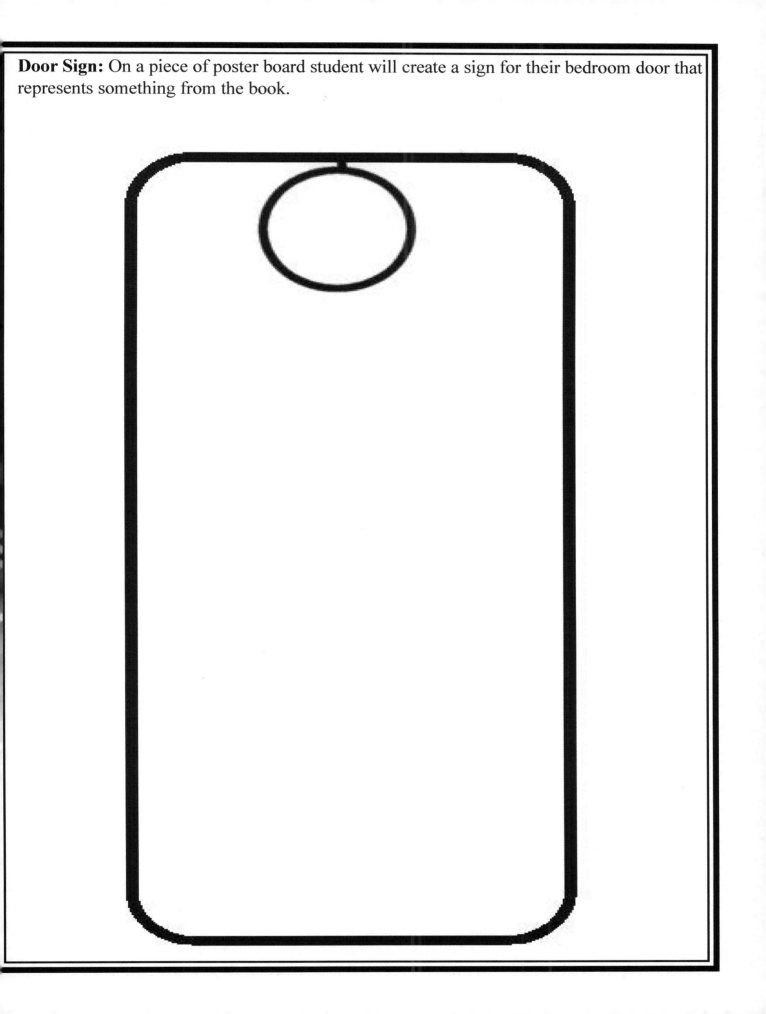

Mini Book : Student will create a mini book that retells the story. This may be put on the Lapbook.

12

1

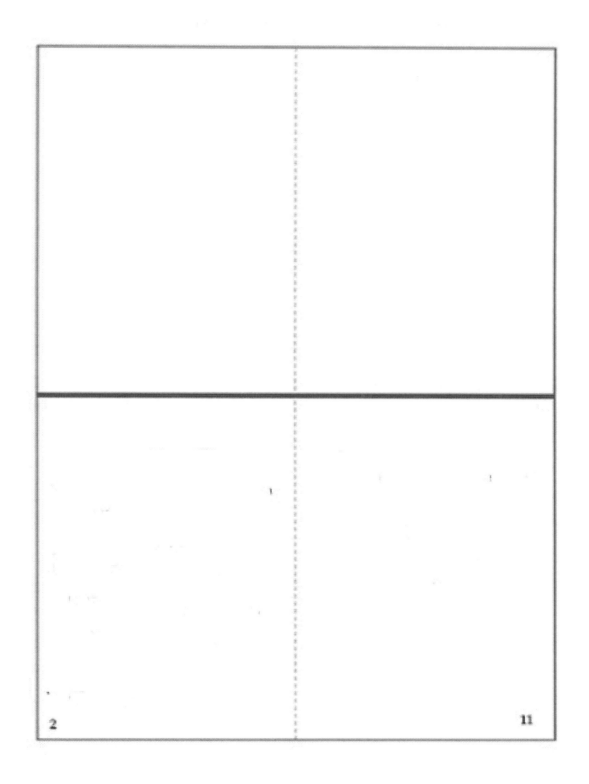

2

11

Print double sided.   Cut on the red lines.   Fold on the dotted lines.

10

3

8

5

Print double sided. Cut on the red lines. Fold on the dotted lines.

4

9

6

7

Lesson 10
Activities

Lesson 10 Activities: Students will use the book they are studying and information found on the internet for the following activities. Then the student will write the information required for this activity on the patterns or in their notebook. The patterns may be cut out and placed on the lapbook.

Encyclopedia:
Student will choose one subject from this lesson that interested them and look it up on the internet or in encyclopedia. They will write the name of the subject across the top of the monitor pattern. On the monitor screen section, they will write three or more interesting facts about the subject.

Journal:
Student will imagine that they are one of the characters from the story. After reading each lesson, they will write a short journal entry telling what happened from that character's point of view.
Student will also draw a picture to go along with the journal entry.
At the end of the book, student will staple all the journal entries together to form a complete booklet.
They can even create a special cover for it from construction paper.

Vocabulary word: _____

Definition of the word: _____
_____
_____

Antonym of the word: _____
How many syllables does the word have? _____

Vocabulary Word: _____
Sentence using the word: _____
_____
_____

Synonym of the word: _____

Vocabulary: Student will use the vocabulary words from the list for this lesson. On one of the patterns, or on one index card they will write one vocabulary word. They should also write the definition of the word, then the Antonym and how many Syllables the word has.

On the other card, the student will write the same word. They will write a full sentence using this word and then write the Synonym of the word.

They will repeat this for all the vocabulary words in this lesson.

Place the patterns or cards in an envelope which can be glued into the student's notebook or onto the lapbook..

Sequencing: At the end of the lesson the student will write two of the main events on these two strips. Save them in an envelope which can be glued onto the lapbook or in the notebook. At the end of the book, these strips can be taken out and the student can arrange them in the correct order as they occurred in the story.

_____
_____
_____
_____
_____
_____

Handwriting: Student will pick their favorite sentence that they read in this lesson. Have them write the sentence in their best handwriting on this page or in their notebook.

Student will write out the answers for the following:
Main Idea: In a sentence or two, write what the main idea was of this section.

_____
_____
_____
_____
_____

Key Event: In a sentence or two write what the most important event was in this section.

_____
_____
_____
_____
_____
_____

Prediction: In a sentence of two write what you Predict will happen in the next section.

_____
_____
_____
_____
_____
_____

Comparison: In a sentence of two compare two things in this section. Tell what makes them alike and what makes them different.

_____
_____
_____
_____
_____

Fact or Opinion: In one sentence write a fact about this section and one sentence that is an opinion about the lesson.

_____
_____
_____
_____
_____

Hero vs. Villain: Most stories usually have a hero (the main character) and a villain. The villain may not seem that bad. The villain is usually the character who stands in the way of the main character, or against the main character. Student will name the Hero and the Villain and fill in the "What the Villain does...." square.

Hero

What the Villain does
to hinder the Hero.

Villain

Poetry Form: Student will write a poem about the book or characters using this format.

Shape Poem: To be done on a separate sheet of paper. Shape poems can be made by placing words, which describe a particular object, in such a way that they form the shape of the object. Student will start by making a simple outline of the shape or object (an animal, a football, a fruit etc.) large enough to fill a piece of paper. Then student will brainstorm a minimum of ten words and phrases that describe the shape including action and feeling words as well. Next, student will place a piece of paper over the shape and decide where the words are going to be placed so that they outline the shape but also fit well together. Separate words and phrases with commas. Shape poems can also be created by simply filling in the shape with a poem, as well.

Newspaper Activity:
Student will use this form to write their newspaper piece on then paste it onto their newspaper lay out poster.

Word Search Section: Find all the words

```
Y T A W W K L S Y E T Y P H U S Y G B B
I L I C C G C U T L L S T O U T L Y L R
Y T G A K O J A F T N N E K F H L A U E
S L W N R N C O N T E M P T U O U S N E
E H T N I I O A H C N R E M X K F T D C
T S F N R R L W I N O E I L C K N R E H
T U U T A A E F L C N L S O O E I N R C
L S N S H T I D L E I Y L E I S A O B L
E I E C P N C A L A D H C T R P D I U O
M P N T G I I U T I C G A A R C S T S T
E O A A O M C I L T W P E O K F I A S H
N Z M N E R O I A E M E P D R E D R L Q
T R D D I N P M O I R R B U S T L I N G
Y L E T A C I R T N I E S I V O R P M I
A E L B I S N E H E R P M O C N I S P P
D N E F F R A N T I C A L L Y V K N G E
Z C O N S C I O U S U B S T A N T I A L
D E S P A I R D E D N U O F B M U D P T
E G A V A S N O I T A R I M D A K E G S
R E S E N T M E N T G N I H C E E S E B
```

ACKNOWLEDGED   ADMIRATION   ADZ
BESEECHING   BEWILDERINGLY   BLUNDERBUSS
BREECHCLOTH   BUSTLING   CONSCIOUS
CONTEMPTUOUS   DESPAIR   DISDAINFULLY
DUMBFOUNDED   FEND   FRANTICALLY
HUMILIATION   IMPATIENT   IMPROVISE
INCOMPREHENSIBLE   INSPIRATION   INTRICATE
INTRICATELY   JOHNNYCAKE   KEG
MAGNIFICENT   MATCHLOCK   NONCHALANTLY
PANIC   PELTS   PROCLAIMED   PROPRIETORS
PROTEST   RELUCTANTLY   RESENTFUL
RESENTMENT   SAVAGE   SCORNFUL
SETTLEMENT   SOLEMNLY   STOUTLY
SUBSTANTIAL   SUSPICION   THWACK
TYPHUS   WITS

Creative Writing Activity: A Different End: Student will write a different ending for the story.

Writing Skills Activity: Plot Analysis Board

Student will create this by following the directions.

What you need:
Index Cards, Pictures from the internet, Markers, Crayons. Glue

1. Fold the poster board in half so that it makes a folder.
2. Decorate the front of the folder with pictures and information that includes the Title, the Author, the Illustrator, and the Publisher.
3. On index cards, write the information requested below. Glue the index cards inside the folder. You can put pictures on the cards to go along with them.

   Information to put on cards:
   1. Main Character and Character Traits
   2. Main Setting
   3. Other Characters
   4. Other Settings in the Story
   5. Main Problem
   6. Other Problems
   7. Climax
   8. Solution to the Problem
   9. Your favorite part of the story
   10. What you would change if you could about the story.

Lapbook Activity: The Commandments:
Student will cut out the patter and fold so that the Ten Commandments are on the front. Inside student will write how a character may have broken or upheld one or more of these commandments. Attach to Lapbook.

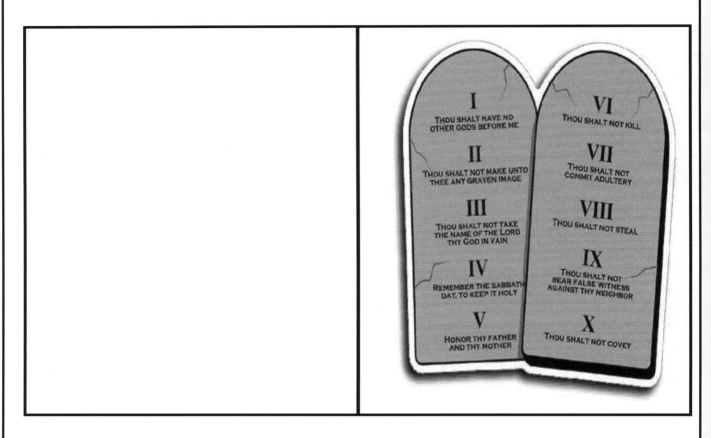

Poster Board Activity:
Jeopardy
On the poster board student will create a game board like the one on the next page. They will cut out several sets of the play money. The teacher will write 4 to 8 questions for each category. The student then picks one category and the dollar amount of the question they will try and answer. The teacher or student reads the question. If the answer is correct the student wins the amount of money that they chose. The next player takes a turn. The winner is the one with the most

Creative Art Activity:
Sketch
Student will imagine they are a sketch artist and using black pencils or charcoal pencils, they will sketch some of the main characters, places or events from the story.

JEOPARDY

People	Places	Animals	Other
$100	$100	$100	$100
$200	$200	$200	$200
$300	$300	$300	$300
$400	$400	$400	$400

Additional Activities

Additional Writing Activities

Imaginative: Imaginative writing is when you write a fanciful story using your imagination. Student will write one that comes to mind while they read this book.

Essay: An essay is a short piece of writing, from an author's personal point of view. Student will write a short essay from their point of view about a subject that comes to mind while reading these books.

Speech: A speech is the act of delivering a formal spoken communication to an audience . Student will write a short speech that one of the characters from the books may have given.

Autobiography: An autobiography is a story of a person's life. Student will write a short autobiography outline of one of the characters or they could write about the author as well.

Humor: Humor allows the reader to laugh and enjoy a story. Student will write a humorous piece about a subject or thing mentioned in these books.

ABC Story: ABC Stories are short stories that have each sentence starting with the next letter in the alphabet. Student will write a short ABC story about an event or one of the characters in the book. For example:
 A girl named Kit lived in America. By noon she was happy...

Literature Web: A story will make you think of many things and feel many things. Student will draw this chart in their notebook and fill it in.

Key Words: What were some important words or phrases?

Feelings: What feelings did you have while reading the book?

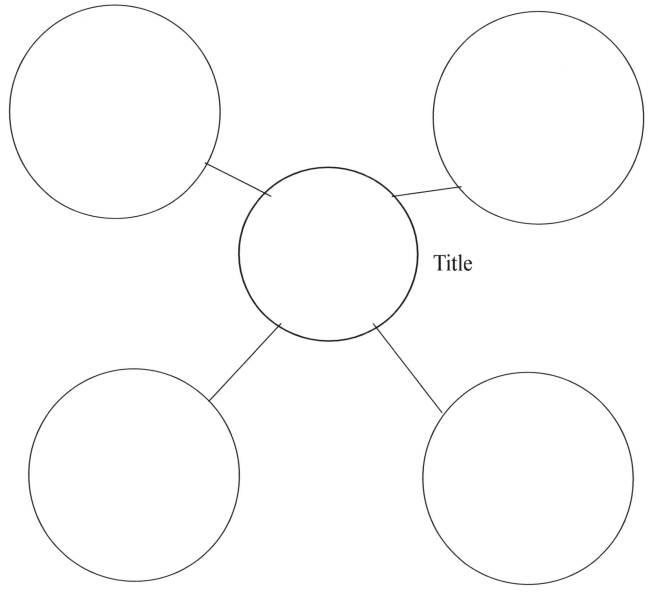

Title

Symbols: Did the author use any symbols in the story?

Attitude: What do you think the authors attitude is about the subject this story is about?

Sign Language:

On a piece of poster board, student will glue a larger versions of the sign language alphabet. Now the teacher will sign a name, scene or vocabulary word from the story. Students try to figure the word out by pointing to the correct sign language letter and spelling out the words.

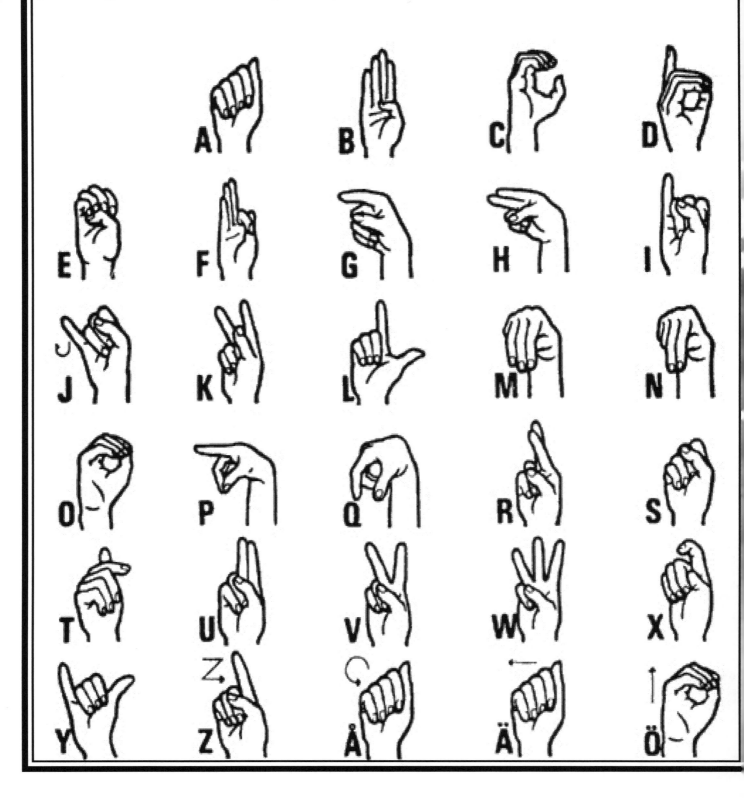

Theater Box:

Get a cardboard box with a flat side larger than a piece of paper. In the side cut out a square about 6 by 9 inches. This will be the opening for your theater.

While reading each chapter of the book, Student will draw one or more of the main scenes on 8 1/2 by 11 inch drawing paper. Stay within the inner 6 by 9 inches though. Color these with markers, paint, colored pencils etc.

Figure out a way that these pictures can be slid in and out of the box, so they appear in the opening and it looks like you are changing scenes, or draw them all on one long roll, and create rollers in each end of the box out of paper towel rolls.

At the end of the book you should have a whole story in these scenes. Present the scenes in your theater to family or friends. You will have to act as the announcer and explain the main events in each scene.

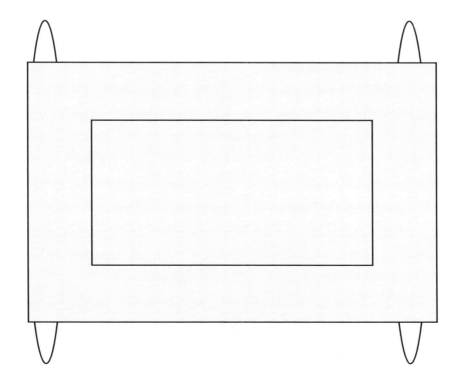

Acting: Student will

1. Dress up as one of the characters in the story. They can act out their favorite part of the story.
2. Host a talk show where another member of the family acts as the television host. Your student is the main character of the story. They ask you questions about the story.
3. Hold a trial. Someone dresses up as the villain in the story. Someone dresses up as the main character. Someone as a lawyer and someone as a judge. Hold a trial to determine if the villain is really guilty of crimes or not.

Rock Art:
Student will gather smooth rocks of different shapes and sizes. Student will clean the rocks and when dry create characters from the book with the rocks, by painting them, making clothes for them and gluing on google eyes.

Name Art:
Student will write the main characters name in the middle of 1/4 poster board and then decorate all around it in any art form they like.

Carving:

Use soap or wax and carve a character from the story. All you need to carve soap is a bar of soap and a spoon. If your child is old enough to use a butter knife then you can let them have a butter knife to carve their soap with. Soap carving can be messy so it is best to be done on a table covered with an old cloth or newspaper. And everyone doing the carving should have old clothes on.

When carving soap, you can use any size bar of soap you would like, but a nice big bar of soap is better to get creative with. If you are lucky enough to have a bar of home made lye soap that will work as well. Unwrap your bar of soap and decide what you want to make with your bar of soap. Soap is a soft material so a spoon will work to carve a bar of soap just fine. A knife can give your bar of soap more detail then a spoon can but it is more dangerous.

Sewing:

Use felt and material stuffing. Create a pattern for something from the story such as an animal or character. Cut out two of the same patterns from the felt. Have student sew around the outside edges. Stuff with stuffing and complete the sewing.

Design a Needlepoint:
Get graph paper and have student design a needlepoint by placing an x in the boxes to design the picture.

Shape Puzzle: On poster board student will draw out a large copy of the shape of a character or item from the book. Cut it into a puzzle pattern.

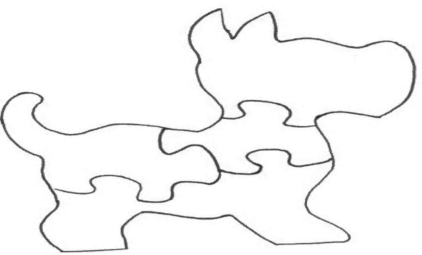

I Spy

Student will find pictures on the internet of things that come to mind while reading this book. Pictures of the characters, of the vocabulary words etc. Student will print and then glue them all over the poster board. Now they should make an I spy set of calling cards on index cards.

For example your cards would say:

I spy a cat.

I spy a rat.

Give the cards to a younger child and see if they can find all the items on the I spy poster.

Bingo: Print as many of these Bingo boards as you need for the students. Write the vocabulary words in the squares of the Bingo boards. Each board should be different. Use the definition index cards as the call cards for the game.

B	I	N	G	O
		Free Space		

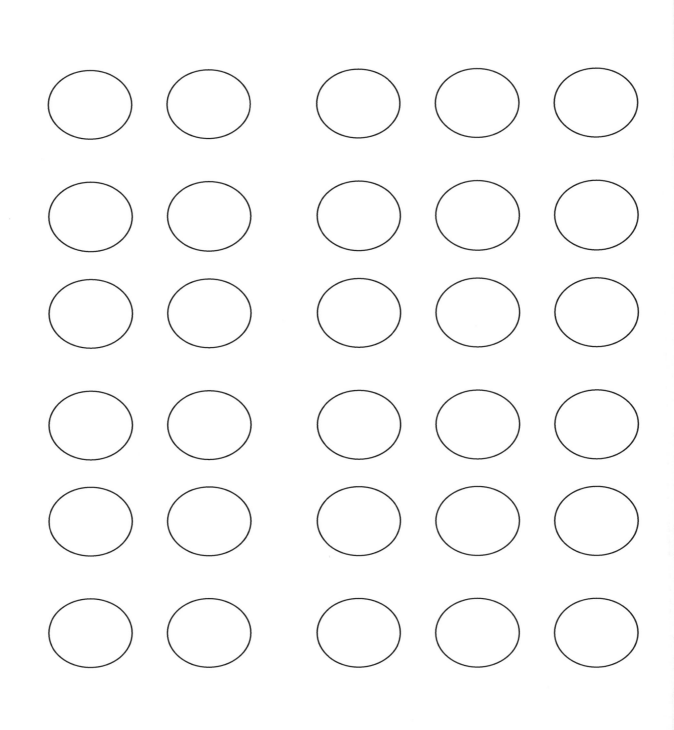

Comprehension

The following pages have the
Fill in the Blanks,
True and False,
Multiple Choice
and
Who, What, Where, When,
Why and How Questions
for all lessons.

Use the Vocabulary words
on the following page for the
questions

Lesson 1   Chapter 1,2,3
Lesson 2   Chapter 4,5
Lesson 3   Chapter 6,7,8
Lesson 4   Chapter 9,10
Lesson 5   Chapter 11,12,13
Lesson 6   Chapter 14,15
Lesson 7   Chapter 16,17,18
Lesson 8   Chapter 19,20
Lesson 9   Chapter 21,22,23
Lesson 10   Chapter 24,25

Vocabulary Words:

Lesson 1.   puncheon   blunderbuss   matchlock   johnnycake   chinking   proprietors   settlement   deacon   redskins   pelts

Lesson 2.   sensible   precious   molasses   persuaded   conscious   wits   protest   panic   keg   pewter

Lesson 3.   resentful   despair   disdainfully   scornful   savage   adz   primer   detested   incomprehensible   impatient

Lesson 4.   nonchalantly   dumbfounded   sapling   admiration   resigned   contemptuous   suspicion   solemnly   horrid   resentment

Lesson 5.   superior   acknowledged   envious   chagrined   indignant   defiant   inflict   reluctantly   goaded   improvise

Lesson 6.   inspiration   impolite   magnificent   comical   immense   stoutly   intention   tribute   distaste   squaw

Lesson 7.   wig-wams   stockade   array   wampum   pungent   intricate   aping   substantial   relenting   substantial

Lesson 8.   breeches   breechcloth   thwack   resolved   humiliation   disgrace   ordeal   awkwardly   proclaimed   bewilderingly

Lesson 9.   reproach   soberly   persisted   anxious   beseeching   intricately   treaties   impressed   deceived   tramped

Lesson 10. floundered   typhus   hereabouts   fend   marveled   cloak   bustling   frantically   plunder   musket

Lesson 1   Chapters 1, 2, 3

Fill in the Blanks: Write the vocabulary word that best completes the sentence.
Words: deacon   puncheon   chinking   proprietors

1. Inside the cabin there was a sturdy _____ table in the corner.
2. He had been assured by the _____ that his settlement would be safe.
3. _____ the spaces between the logs was an endless task.
4. The man was greeted like a _____ in his community.

True / False: Write T if statement is true; write F if it is false.
1. _____ Matt felt like someone was watching him in the woods.
2. _____ Matt invited Ben to stay with him.
3. _____ Ben had stolen Matt's rifle.
4. _____ Matt shot a raccoon and made a delicious stew.

Multiple Choice: Write ABCD in the space for the best answer.

1. _____ Matt would be _____ years old by the time his family got to Maine.
A.10
B.13
C.12
D.18

2. _____ Most of the Indians in Maine had left the area to live in _____.
A. New York
B. California
C. Mexico
D. Canada

3._____ When the bugs are bad the Indians would camp near the _____.
A. river
B. town
C. coast
D. mountains

4._____ Matt's father said to be _____ to the Indians if he met them.
A. polite
B. disrespectful
C. rough
D. nasty

Lesson 1
Write full sentences for this section:

1. Who would be the first settlers in a new township in Maine?
2. What kind of chores did Matt have to do while his father was gone?
3. Where had Ben come from?
4. When Matt and his father reached Maine what did they do?
5. Why did Matt's father go back to Massachusetts?
6. How many weeks would Matt's father be gone?

(Who) _____
_____
_____
_____

(What)_____
_____
_____
_____

(Where)_____
_____
_____
_____

(When)_____
_____
_____
_____

(Why)_____
_____
_____
_____

(How)_____
_____
_____
_____

Lesson 2   Chapters 4, 5
Fill in the Blanks: Write the vocabulary word that best completes the sentence.
Words: keg   persuaded   panic   precious

1. Matt began to _____ when he saw the bear.
2. Molasses was a _____ part of every meal.
3. The large _____was upside on the floor.
4. Matt's mother _____ them to bring molasses.

True / False: Write T if statement is true; write F if it is false.
1. _____ There were plenty of bees in America before the English colonists came.
2. _____ Matt got stung by one bee
3. _____ The Indian said bee needles have poison in them.
4. _____ Matt remained afraid of the Indian as he cared for him.

Multiple Choice: Write ABCD in the space for the best answer.

1. _____ The _____ colonist brought bees to America.
A. Spanish
B. French
C. English
D. Japanese

2. _____ Matt's skin felt like it was _____ from head to toe after the bees stung him.
A. going numb
B. on fire
C. freezing
D. peeling

3. _____ The elderly Indian was very _____ with Matt.
A. angry
B. clumsy
C. rough
D. gentle

4. _____ To stop the bees from stinging Matt jumped into the _____.
A. pond
B. ocean
C. mud
D. bushes

Lesson 2
Write full sentences for this section:

1. Who lifted Matt out of the pond?
2. What did Matt decide to do one morning?
3. Where did the Indian take Matt?
4. When Matt came back from fishing what condition was the cabin in?
5. Why had Matt almost drowned?
6. How did the elderly Indian care for Matt?

(Who) _____
_____
_____
_____

(What)_____
_____
_____
_____

(Where)_____
_____
_____
_____

(When)_____
_____
_____
_____

(Why)_____
_____
_____
_____

(How)_____
_____
_____
_____

Lesson 3   Chapters 6, 7, 8

Fill in the Blanks: Write the vocabulary word that best completes the sentence.
Words: adz   disdainfully   savage   primer

1. There was nothing _____ about Saknis and Attean.
2. Matt could still see the brown colored _____ in his mother's hands as she taught him.
3. Matt and his father came to Maine with an axe and an _____.
4. Attean swung the dead rabbit _____ on the table.

True / False: Write T if statement is true; write F if it is false.
1. _____ Saknis fed Matt stew and cornbread.
2. _____ Attean was glad his grandfather wanted him to learn to read.
3. _____ Matt greeted Saknis respectfully.
4. _____ Attean told Matt that the white man's book was foolish.

Multiple Choice: Write ABCD in the space for the best answer.

1. _____ Saknis brought Matt a new pair of _____.
A. socks
B. gloves
C. moccasins
D. boots

2. _____ Attean left the cabin when Matt told him it could take _____ to learn to read.
A. a month
B. two years
C. a year
D. seven days

3._____ Matt was _____ that Saknis found him when he did.
A. unhappy
B. embarrassed
C. grateful
D. angry

4._____ Attean was _____ years old.
A. nine
B. fifteen
C. ten
D. fourteen

Lesson 3
Write full sentences for this section:

1. Who is Saknis?
2. What family or clan did Saknis belong to?
3. Where did Saknis get the moccassins?
4. When Matt gave Saknis his book what did Saknis do?
5. Why did Matt give Saknis his Robinson Crusoe book?
6. How did Matt know that Saknis had been watching him in the forest?

(Who) _____
_____
_____
_____

(What)_____
_____
_____
_____

(Where)_____
_____
_____
_____

(When)_____
_____
_____
_____

(Why)_____
_____
_____
_____

(How)_____
_____
_____
_____

Lesson 4   Chapters 9, 10

Fill in the Blanks: Write the vocabulary word that best completes the sentence.
Words: contemptuous   admiration   horrid   nonchalantly

1. Attean had a _____ grin on his face when Matt tripped and fell.
2. Matt watched in _____ as Attean hunted without the use of a gun.
3. Attean was _____, the whole matter of white man's words were nonsense to him.
4. Matt swung his catch _____ across the table as Attean had.

True / False: Write T if statement is true; write F if it is false.
1. _____ Attean was disappointed when Matt learned to catch food with a snare.
2. _____ Matt refused to stick with the treaty after he learned how to hunt without his rifle.
3. _____ Attean took Matt by surprise when he asked him to go fishing?
4. _____ Matt lost his footing and slipped into the water as he tried to spear a fish.

Multiple Choice: Write ABCD in the space for the best answer.

1. _____ Attean used a _____ to catch fish.
A. fishing pole
B. bluderbuss
C. spear
D. knife

2. _____ Attean made Matt a fishing hook out of a _____.
A. dear antler
B. maple sapling
C. pewter spoon
D. seashell

3. _____ Matt and Attean cooked their fish on _____ held over the fire.
A. rope
B. pots
C. rocks
D. sticks

4. _____ Attean's pouch is made out of what?
A. muskrat skin
B. deer skin
C. cotton
D. fur

Lesson 4
Write full sentences for this section:

1. Who proved to Matt he didn't always have to depend on white man's tools?
2. What did Attean feel bound to do?
3. Where had Matt found a partridge?
4. When Matt looked at the fish hook that Attean made him he realized what?
5. Why did Attean abruptly leave in the middle of the story?
6. How does Attean catch rabbits without a rifle or bow and arrow?

(Who) _____
_____
_____
_____

(What)_____
_____
_____
_____

(Where)_____
_____
_____
_____

(When)_____
_____
_____
_____

(Why)_____
_____
_____
_____

(How)_____
_____
_____
_____

Lesson 5   Chapters 11, 12, 13

Fill in the Blanks: Write the vocabulary word that best completes the sentence.
Words: goaded   chagrined   inflict   reluctantly

1. Attean _____ listened as Matt continued on with the story.
2. Matt did not like to _____ pain on any living creature.
3. Matt was constantly _____ to keep trying to win Attean's respect.
4. Matt was _____ when Attean came out of the woods and caught him target practicing.

True / False: Write T if statement is true; write F if it is false.
1. _____ Matt trusted Attean but didn't really like him.
2. _____ A beaver was carved on a tree near the beaver dam.
3. _____ Attean refused to teach Matt how to not get lost in the forest.
4. _____ The carved beaver was a sign that belonged to Attean's tribe.

Multiple Choice: Write ABCD in the space for the best answer.

1. _____ Matt wished he could win Attean's _____ .
A. trust
B. support
C. respect
D. approval

2. _____ Matt decided one morning that he must have a _____ .
A. horse
B. bow
C. wagon
D. tomahawk

3._____ Attean's grandfather would not allow the Beaver clan to buy _____ .
A. molasses
B. rifles
C. flour
D. iron traps

4._____ Attean said white man hunted moose and beaver just for their _____ .
A. skin
B. teeth
C. hooves
D. meat

Lesson 5
Write full sentences for this section:

1. Who did Matt and Attean find one morning in the forest?
2. What did Attean leave in the forest as he walked through it?
3. Where did Matt look for Indian signs?
4. When Indians killed an animal for food they also did what with it?
5. Why did Attean not release the fox from the trap?
6. How had Attean become Matt's teacher?

(Who) _____

_____

_____

_____

(What)_____

_____

_____

_____

(Where)_____

_____

_____

_____

(When)_____

_____

_____

_____

(Why)_____

_____

_____

_____

(How)_____

_____

_____

_____

Lesson 6   Chapters 14, 15

Fill in the Blanks: Write the vocabulary word that best completes the sentence.
Words: comical   immense   tribute   squaw

1. Attean asked a _____ to cut the meat.
2. The bear cub had a _____ head.
3. The she-bear had _____ claws.
4. Matt remembered the Indian boy's _____.

True / False: Write T if statement is true; write F if it is false.
1. _____ Indians did not kill animals for sport and anything killed would be used.
2. _____ The men of the clan did the hunting, while the squaws cut and carried the meat.
3. _____ Matt and Attean encountered a panther in the forest.
4. _____ As soon as Matt saw what had come out of the bushes he ran as fast as he could.

Multiple Choice: Write ABCD in the space for the best answer.

1. _____ Attean told Matt that he had moved quick like a _____.
A. wolf
B. fox
C. Indian
D. bee

2. _____ Matt had sensed not to _____ when he saw the bear.
A. run
B. yell
C. sing
D. dance

3. _____ Gluskabe made _____.
A. all Indians
B. all animals
C. thunder
D. all of the above

4. _____ Attean was _____ when Robinson Crusoe was done.
A. happy
B. disappointed
C. mad
D. indifferent

Lesson 6
Write full sentences for this section:

1. Whom did Attean say Gluskabe was?
2. What story did Attean tell Matt about?
3. Where did Attean go after killing the bear?
4. When Robinson Crusoe was done where did Matt decide to get his next adventure stories?
5. Why did Attean speak slowly and solemnly to the bear after killing it?
6. How did Matt feel when he looked at the dead bear after Attean left?

(Who) _____
_____
_____
_____

(What)_____
_____
_____
_____

(Where)_____
_____
_____
_____

(When)_____
_____
_____
_____

(Why)_____
_____
_____
_____

(How)_____
_____
_____
_____

Lesson 7   Chapters 16, 17, 18

Fill in the Blanks: Write the vocabulary word that best completes the sentence.
Words: stockade   substantial   wig-wams   pungent

1. Attean's grandmother applied a _____ smelling paste to Matt's wound.
2. The frenzied dogs burst through the _____ and rushed towards Matt.
3. Cone-shaped _____ filled the Indian village.
4. The bear could provide a _____ amount of food for the clan.

True / False: Write T if statement is true; write F if it is false.
1. _____ The squaws made a feast with the bear that Attean killed.
2. _____ When Attean came to fetch Matt he was covered in war paint.
3. _____ Attean's village refused to accept Matt at their feast.
4. _____ Attean's grandmother did not want Attean at the feast.

Multiple Choice: Write ABCD in the space for the best answer.

1. _____ Saknis had Attean invite Matt to the _____ feast.
A. war feast
B. peace feast
C. bear feast
D. rain feast

2. _____ White men made money by selling _____.
A. deer antlers
B. Indian scalps
C. moccasins
D. medicinal plants

3. _____ Saknis said that Indians must learn to _____ with white man.
A. eat
B. sing
C. sang
D. live

4. _____ Who helped Matt to free Attean's dog?
A. Attean's sister Marie
B. Attean's grandmother
C. Ben
D. Saknis

Lesson 7
Write full sentences for this section:

1. Who had killed Attean's mother for her scalp?
2. What had happened to Attean's father?
3. Where did Matt get help to free Attean's dog?
4. When Matt had wondered into Turtle territory what did he find?
5. Why was Matt worried when he counted his ten notched sticks?
6. How did Attean's grandmother react when she saw Matt's torn hand?

(Who) _____
_____
_____
_____

(What)_____
_____
_____
_____

(Where)_____
_____
_____
_____

(When)_____
_____
_____
_____

(Why)_____
_____
_____
_____

(How)_____
_____
_____
_____

Lesson 8   Chapters 19, 20

Fill in the Blanks: Write the vocabulary word that best completes the sentence.
Words: breeches   resolved   ordeal   proclaimed

1. Matt was _____ to learn more of the Indian ways.
2. English _____ were tight and uncomfortable.
3. Matt was _____ the winner of every game.
4. Attean's dog had gone through a painful _____.

True / False: Write T if statement is true; write F if it is false.
1. _____ Matt wanted to learn many things as he curiously watched the squaws work.
2. _____ If Attean finds his manitou he could become a hunter and go with the men.
3. _____ The Indian boys of the village refused to let Matt play their games.
4. _____ Attean was afraid of not finding his manitou.

Multiple Choice: Write ABCD in the space for the best answer.

1. _____ The women spread _____ on bark to dry in the sun.
A. mud
B. leather
C. berries
D. stones

2. _____ Matt watched as the Indian women pounded dry _____ into course flour.
A. dried wheat berries
B. clams
C. dried berries
D. dried corn kernels

3. _____ For Attean to not find his manitou it would be viewed as _____.
A. a disgrace
B. shameful
C. a relief
D. both A and B

4. _____ If Attean found his manitou it would be the end of his and Matt's _____.
A. adventures
B. friendship
C. hope
D. happiness

Lesson 8
Write full sentences for this section:

1. Who was going to learn to find their manitou?
2. What did Matt feel after he spent a day with Attean at his village?
3. Where would Attean go to find his manitou?
4. When Matt sat in the canoe what did Attean's dog do?
5. Why did Attean's grandmother invite Matt to the village?
6. How did Attean explain what a manitou was to Matt?

(Who) _____
_____
_____
_____

(What)_____
_____
_____
_____

(Where)_____
_____
_____
_____

(When)_____
_____
_____
_____

(Why)_____
_____
_____
_____

(How)_____
_____
_____
_____

Lesson 9   Chapters 21, 22, 23

Fill in the Blanks: Write the vocabulary word that best completes the sentence.
Words: beseeching   anxious   intricately   meager

1. Matt's _____ harvest was safely stored away before the winter.
2. Matt was _____ to see his family.
3. The logs were _____ balanced so they would not fall.
4. Matt could not resist the dog's _____ eyes.

True / False: Write T if statement is true; write F if it is false.
1. _____ Attean gave his dog to Matt as a gift.
2. _____ Medabe means white warrior.
3. _____ Attean was pleased and impressed with the watch that Matt gave him.
4. _____ Matt made a hat out of an otter's pelt and mittens from two rabbit skins.

Multiple Choice: Write ABCD in the space for the best answer.

1. _____ Matt took care of his harvest by shucking the corn and hanging strips of _____ to dry.
A. pumpkin
B. beans
C. eggplant
D. zucchini

2. _____ Saknis said Matt and Attean would be like _____.
A. brothers
B. friends
C. enemies
D. strangers

3. _____ Saknis said he would be glad to have Matt as his _____.
A. wigwam
B. wampum
C. manitou
D. nkweniss

4. _____ What gift did Atteans's grandfather give Matt?
A. snowshoes
B. knife
C. sled
D. rifle

Lesson 9
Write full sentences for this section:

1. Who did Attean refer to as medabe?
2. What had Matt finally gained by waiting at the cabin for his family to arrive?
3. Where were the Indians going now that fall had come?
4. When Matt mentioned to Attean about coming back in the spring what was Attean's reply?
5. Why did Saknis invite Matt to go with them?
6. How did Matt now feel about Indians?

(Who) _____

_____

_____

(What)_____

_____

_____

_____

(Where)_____

_____

_____

_____

(When)_____

_____

_____

_____

(Why)_____

_____

_____

_____

(How)_____

_____

_____

Fill in the Blanks: Write the vocabulary word that best completes the sentence.
Words: floundered   fend   marveled   typhus

1. Many villagers got sick with _____.
2. The dog _____ happily behind Matt?
3. Matt's father _____ at all the work he had done maintaining the cabin.
4. Matt was able to _____ for himself.

True / False: Write T if statement is true; write F if it is false.
1. _____ Matt's father was angry that Matt had dealt with the Indians.
2. _____ Matt's baby sibling had only lived five days after being born.
3. _____ Saknis had been right, more white men were coming.
4. _____ Matt's sister Sarah died from typhus.

Multiple Choice: Write ABCD in the space for the best answer.

1. _____ Matt's mother was determined to make it to the cabin before _____.
A. Thanksgiving
B. Christmas
C. New Years Day
D. April Fools Day

2. _____ Matt made himself a tea made of _____.
A. raspberry leaves
B. dandelion roots
C. hemlock tips
D. bark

3. _____ Matt proudly told his family that he had _____.
A. Indian friends
B. an Indian brother
C. found his manitou
D. both A and B

4. _____ Matt's mother _____ as she looked around the cabin.
A. admired everything
B. became disgusted
C. grew fearful
D. jumped for joy

Lesson 10
Write full sentences for this section:

1. Whom did Matt see dragging a sled along the frozen stream?
2. What did Matt feel as he stood looking up at the sky?
3. Where did Matt's new neighbors have a cabin?
4. When Matt and his father were unpacking the sled what did his father tell him?
5. Why had Matt's family arrived late to the cabin?
6. How did Matt's snowshoes make him feel?

(Who) _____
_____
_____
_____

(What)_____
_____
_____
_____

(Where)_____
_____
_____
_____

(When)_____
_____
_____
_____

(Why)_____
_____
_____
_____

(How)_____
_____
_____
_____

Answer Key

Lesson 1

Fill in the Blanks
1. puncheon
2. proprietors
3. chinking
4. deacon

True and False
1. T
2. F
3. T
4. F

Multiple Choice
1. B
2. D
3. C
4. A

Comprehension
1. Matt and his family
2. Chinking the spaces between the cabin logs with clay, cut down trees for wood, water the corn patch
3. Penobscot River
4. They claimed their plot of land and cleared a patch to build their cabin on and plant corn
5. To bring Matt's mother and sister Sarah, and new born baby to Maine
6. six to seven weeks

Lesson 2

Fill in the Blanks
1. panic
2. precious
3. keg
4. persuaded

True and False
1. F
2. F
3. T
4. F

Multiple Choice
1. C
2. B
3. D
4. A

Comprehension
1. An elderly Indian and Indian boy
2. He decided to climb a tree and get a cupful of honey
3. Back to his cabin
4. The door was broken, flour was spilled all over the floor, and the molasses keg was empty
5. His feet became tangled in dragging weeds
6. He gave him some bitter tasting medicine

Lesson 3
Fill in the Blanks
1. savage
2. primer
3. adz
4. disdainfully
True and False
1. T
2. F
3. T
4. T
Multiple Choice
1. C
2. C
3. C
4. D
Comprehension
1. The elderly Indian that helped save Matt's life
2. He belonged to the family of beaver (Beaver clan)
3. A beaver woman had made them
4. He made a treaty; he asked Matt to teach Attean to read and Attean would hunt and bring him food
5. It was the only thing of value he had besides the Bible
6. He had brought Matt straight home to his cabin
Lesson 4
Fill in the Blanks
1. horrid
2. admiration
3. contemptuous
4. nonchalantly
True and False
1. F
2. F
3. T
4. T
Multiple Choice
1. C
2. B
3. D
4. A
Comprehension
1. Attean
2. He felt bound to keep the terms of his grandfather's treaty with Matt
3. Stuck in one of his snares
4. He would never need to worry about losing a hook because he could make new ones when needed
5. He didn't like that the savage kneeled to the white man, he said it was better to die than be a slave
6. He makes a snare out of a snakelike root and two forked saplings and a branch

Lesson 5
Fill in the Blanks
1. reluctantly
2. inflict
3. goaded
4. chagrined
True and False
1. T
2. T
4. T
Multiple Choice
1. C
2. B
3. D
4. A
Comprehension
1. A fox caught in a white man's trap
2. He left markers so he could find his way back home
3. As he walked through the forest
4. They find a use for every scrap of the animal
5. It was on the land belonging to the Turtle clan
6. He taught Matt how to survive off the land; showed him what to eat and not eat; which plants had medicinal benefits and how to make hunting tools
Lesson 6
Fill in the Blanks
1. squaw
2. comical
3. immense
4. tribute
True and False
1. T
2. T
3. F
4. F
Multiple Choice
1. C
2. A
3. D
4. B
Comprehension
1. He is the Great Spirit that Indians worshiped
2. The Beaver clan have a story somewhat similar to the story of Noah in the Bible
3. Back home to get the squaws so they could cut and carry the meat back home
4. From the Bible
5. He felt bad for having to kill the bear and asked her to forgive him
6. Matt would have like to have a share of the meat or a big claw to show his father

Lesson 7
Fill in the Blanks
1. pungent
2. stockade
3. wig-wams
4. substantial
True and False
1. T
2. F
3. F
4. T
Multiple Choice
1. C
2. B
3. D
4. A
Comprehension
1. White man
2. He went out on a war trail to find the white man that killed Attean's mother
3. He ran back to Attean's village to find him
4. Attean's dog was stuck in a steel trap
5. His sticks showed that August had passed and that September was almost over
6. She grabbed his arm, led him to the cabin, and cleaned and treated his wound
Lesson 8
Fill in the Blanks
1. resolved
2. breeches
3. proclaimed
4. ordeal
True and False
1. T
2. T
3. F
4. T
Multiple Choice
1. C
2. D
3. D
4. A
Comprehension
1. Attean
2. He felt content like he had passed some sort of test in Attean's eyes
3. After special preparation he would go into the forest alone and stay there many days without eating
4. He sat a few inches from Matt's knees and let him pet him, something he wouldn't allow before
5. She was surprised that a white boy would go a long way to help an Indian boy's dog
6. It was like a spirit and could come in many ways-as a bird or animal, a tree, or a voice speaking to him and when a boy finds it he would become a man

Lesson 9
Fill in the Blanks
1. meager
2. anxious
3. intricately
4. beseeching
True and False
1. T
2. T
3. F
4. T
Multiple Choice
1. A
2. A
3. D
4. A
Comprehension
1. Matt
2. Attean's respect
3. All the Indians were going north to hunt moose
4. He said they were going to find new hunting grounds because white man would come soon leaving no where to hunt
5. Matt's father had not returned and snow was soon to come
6. He no longer distrusted them
Lesson 10
Fill in the Blanks
1. typhus
2. floundered
3. marveled
4. fend
True and False
1. F
2. T
3. T
4. F
Multiple Choice
1. B
2. C
3. D
4. A
Comprehension
1. Matt's father
2. He felt snow coming
3. Five miles away
4. He told him that he had done a grown man's job and that he was proud of him
5. They had all gotten sick with typhus
6. He felt happy and free, no longer afraid of the winter ahead

Made in the USA
Las Vegas, NV
05 July 2022

51163379R00081